covet garden
HOME

decor inspiration for telling your own story

covetgarden.com

Cataloguing data available from Library and Archives Canada
978-1-927958-11-7

Printed and bound in Canada by the Lowe-Martin Group
Distributed in Canada by Raincoast
Distributed in the U.S. by Publishers Group West

Cover photographs (clockwise from top left) by Donna Griffith,
Tracy Shumate, Jodi Pudge and Jodi Pudge
Opposite page photograph by Ashley Capp
Back cover photographs by Ashley Capp, Donna Griffith and Jodi Pudge

contact@covetgarden.com
Visit covetgarden.com for monthly home tours and more inspiration.

Figure 1 Publishing Inc.
Vancouver BC Canada
www.figure1pub.com

FIGURE 1 PUBLISHING

Based on the Cascades paper we used to print this publication compared
with products in the industry made with 100% virgin fibre, our savings were

48 trees
3 tennis courts

42 GJ
193,166 60W light
bulbs for one hour

7,001 kg of CO_2
emissions of
2 cars per year

2,131 kg of waste
43 waste containers

173,819 litres of water
497 days of water
consumption

9 kg NO_x
emissions of one
truck during 28 days

FSC® is not responsible for any calculations on saving resources by choosing this paper.

WE ALL LOVE A GOOD STORY

It's one of the reasons we started our online magazine, covetgarden.com, over three years ago—we like to peek behind the curtains and share a moment in the history of a space and the lives of the people who inhabit it.

And over time we realized that as diverse as these stories are, they all fit together to build a bigger narrative: when design is personal, it's much more interesting. Which is why we wanted to dedicate this special print edition, *Covet Garden Home*, to helping you tell your own story with creative design.

Covet Garden Home brings you your favourite interiors from our back issues plus brand-new rooms to illustrate how to adapt your home to your evolving life story. In any good tale, connections are key.

We hope that *Covet Garden Home* is a story you'll revisit for years to come.

CONTENTS

54

92

12

MAKING SPACE FOR LIFE AND WORK

LIVING WITH THE THINGS YOU LOVE

THE COVET GARDEN TEAM
MET WORKING AT A LIFESTYLE
MAGAZINE. THAT PUBLICATION
FOLDED, BUT WE LIKED EACH
OTHER AND DECIDED TO
START A PROJECT TOGETHER.
THE BEST WAY TO COMBINE
ALL OUR PASSIONS WAS
TO CREATE AN INTERIORS
MAGAZINE THAT TOLD A
STORY IN EACH ISSUE — OF
A HOME AND THE PEOPLE
AND THE THINGS INSIDE IT.

a few faves (clockwise from bottom left): Rhonda loved Shaun and Todd's updated Victorian from Issue 38, Jess coveted Janna and Dean's rooftop view from Issue 37, and Lynda was a fan of Vicki's summer garage from Issue 12.

lynda felton
co-editor, content lead, stylist

I have worked in fashion as a buyer and personal shopper, as well as in animation, film, television and floral design. For the past eight years I have been a prop stylist and writer.

I often report on current trends, but I'm especially drawn to things with a story: handmade objects that have lived a life and may look a little rough around the edges—anything from a rusty garden tool to a beautifully hand-embroidered tea towel. With *Covet Garden*, I've seen some interiors that follow trends, some that don't, and many that combine elements of both the old and the new, yet every space is as unique as the people who live in it.

jessica reid
co-editor, creative director

I'm a lover of all things beautiful and an admitted fabric hoarder.

I majored in Japanese studies at university but was feeling restless after a couple of years, so I moved to Tokyo for six months. I felt such a connection to Japan—everything was so beautifully designed and presented. From there, I returned to Canada and got my degree in film production, only to eventually find my happy place doing graphic design and art direction.

Now that I'm a mom, and (thankfully!) my daughter loves to craft, I have a constant companion for my sewing, making, and exploring the world for sources of inspiration.

rhonda riche
co-editor, features editor, writer

I consider myself a student of sorts (although my worst nightmares are still about being back in school). I like to go out and learn about and experience as much of the world as I can. I started out studying fine arts, and I still strive to make a drawing a day. I got into journalism because I was a starving artist who discovered that you could get into concerts free if you reviewed them.

I fear my greatest strength is the ability to shop. Specifically, thrift shopping. I live for the thrill of the hunt. I'm especially proud of my collection of works by artists from the Canadian North. They're small pieces that seem at home in my small home.

Your home is an expression of the way you change and develop in response to life experience: you get a job, perhaps change jobs; you maybe meet a partner; you may have kids; you may decide to live alone. Your narrative is always evolving, and a thoughtful approach to design can help you adapt and change too

HOW YOUR SPACE CHANGES

NOW & THEN

Three years ago, we visited the home of Brendon, Shelley and baby daughter Clover. A lot can happen in three years

photography by Jodi Pudge

"I get real joy from being in the playroom," says Shelley. "I love it when the kids are doing their thing and they forget that I'm in there."

BEFORE
Clover's nursery
before the
arrival of
baby August.

BEFORE
A corner
of Clover's
former
playroom.

left: The rocker
was a side-
walk find that
Shelley covered
in Virginia
Johnson fabric.

WE WANTED TO REVISIT Shelley van
Benschop and Brendon Allen's east-end home for many reasons. It
was one of the first places we shot for *Covet Garden*, and it continues
to be one of the most popular of our back issues.

On our initial visit we knew the house was a work in progress, and
since then the couple has continued to renovate. The biggest
addition to the space was new baby August. And as the family is so
inventive and fun to be around, we were looking forward to hanging out with them again. Three years later, the space looks more
refined, although most of their treasures are still in the house—just
used in different ways.

With a family growing in number (and with the kids becoming more
active and needing more room to range), adaptability was important
in Shelley and Brendon's most recent round of renovations.

AFTER Shelley recovered the rocker from Clover's room and uses it in the master bedroom next to the hanging bassinette.

EVEN THOUGH HE IS still a wee man, August's room holds many memories for the family. Shelley's dad passed away recently, so the couple wanted August to know him through stories and objects. "August's room is very nostalgic for me," says Shelley. "There's lots of my dad so that he'll have a sense of him while he's growing up." She has cleverly integrated vintage boyhood objects in many different ways—for example, by using her dad's old scout badges to decorate the footstool, or by framing an old kit bag found on Etsy.

AFTER
A room of
August's own.

AFTER
Brendon built
the new bed
for Clover
and Shelley
covered it
in treasured
textiles.

FLEXIBILITY WAS THE FOCUS

of Shelley and Brendon's most recent renovations. "When we bought the house," she says, "we thought our stay would be temporary." They couldn't afford to gut the place when they moved in, and since then they've done work every year. The advantage of the incremental approach, says Shelley, is that "the house changes as we change."

The couple love their kids, and many decor choices reflect that bond and attentiveness. "It's so nice to see how Clover grows up into who she is," says Shelley. Clover's big-girl room still has many of the same touches that her nursery had, but books, colourful art by local artists and mementoes of growing-up milestones also help personalize the space.

BEFORE Clover's former playroom (shown here) is now her big-girl bedroom.

BEFORE
The former master bedroom.

AFTER
A new family room and playroom includes a day bed (opposite) for guests.

THE SECOND FLOOR IS the best

example of a fluid and dynamic space. One wall serves a bank of storage as well as a place to exhibit an ever-changing collection of kids' art. Open a door and you'll find each section inside organized by use. Since Shelley lost her upstairs studio space, one section now houses the kids' arts and crafts supplies, another, Shelley's sewing machine, serger and materials. "I don't have a huge space," she says. "But if I need to spread out I can come down to the dining room to work."

The day bed in the playroom folds out to become a king-size bed, making the space a guest room for visitors. Adds Brendon, "We also made more space by using pocket doors."

We like to think that Shelley and Brendon's commitment to living in a flexible space is like writing a family history, in a way. The characters evolve and the action changes, but the location serves as a unifying theme. We can't wait to come back in a few more years to see where this story picks up!

SMALL CHANGES

Greg's Parkdale house may have a little footprint, but it also has a lot of charm and a lot of versatility   photography by **Valerie Wilcox**

Art makes a smaller room feel lively without taking up floor space.

"I lived in eight different places in 10 years before I bought the house," says Greg. "I wanted to have my own space to create a sense of personal history."

Photographer Greg White's small west-end home is one that's seen more changes than most we've featured in *Covet Garden*. When he moved in, he worked on Bay Street and occupied the main floor, while his sister and brother-in-law lived in an upstairs apartment. His relatives eventually relocated, and Greg switched careers, creating a studio in the basement for his photography work. Then an itch to travel led him to convert the space once again, making it more of a pied-à-terre/rental property.

When he was living in his compact house, Greg enjoyed well-made, well-designed furnishings. Not too many. Mostly ones with a story. As his own story is ever changing, he wanted pieces with constant value. If the component parts of a home are thoughtfully chosen, they'll work together no matter what configuration or size of room they find themselves in over time.

Because of his limited space, even Greg's collections had to serve their purpose. His Fire King coffee mugs and fromage-festooned cheese plate, for example, got regular use—and his admirable adaptability extends to prized objects, too: "They're beautiful, but I use them. If I break something, I'll get another one."

functions and relations

For a small space not to seem cluttered, it's important to make even functional furnishings feel like objets d'art. Here are three ways Greg turned utilitarian things into conversation pieces.

- **Free up floor space.** Greg knocked down some walls and replaced a swing-out closet door with a sliding barn door made from salvaged wood.

- **Upcycle away.** The enamel sink was found at an antique market for a steal and set on a stand of Greg's devising. "I took a woodworking course," he says. "It gave me the confidence to build things."

- **Add some character.** The fireplace doesn't function, so Greg used the mantel to display art and antique treasures and add some warmth to the room.

"We don't have a cottage to escape to," says Jen. "But recreating that feeling was my goal."

NATURALLY RESOURCEFUL

Jen and Aaron took their inspiration from the great outdoors to create a laid-back first-floor living space **photography by Jodi Pudge**

W hat appealed to us about filmmaker Aaron Woodley and costumer Jen Evans's house is that it demonstrates that when you have a growing family, you don't need to move to a bigger house, you just have to be a little more inventive with your floor plan. To come up with a space that would accommodate kids, family and friends, Jen decided to look to her own childhood for ideas.

"I'm from the West Coast—Victoria, BC," says Jen. "When we did our reno, I was definitely channelling that.

"What we really needed was a family room," she says. Because the neighbourhood was built on a creek bed, most of the homes in the area have flooding problems, so they didn't want to build in the basement. Plus, she says, "We wanted a family space that was part of our whole living space—not the kids sequestered on a whole other floor."

The solution was to build a family room off the kitchen. "I grew up with a sunken living room," says Jen to account for the space's step-down design. "When I'm cooking dinner I can see the kids playing."

Both Jen and Aaron love to cook, so the kitchen was another big part of the recent renovations. "It's the centre of the house," says Aaron. The layout and design are both quite simple, with no interruption in the flow of the main floor from kitchen to dining area to family room. And, he adds, "you can get a nice view from all angles."

store your nuts

Two ways to make your space more versatile:

- **Be practical.** With kids, kid stuff is going to show up all over the house. If you do a one-stop shop for storage, bedding and toys at a bigger chain store, not only can you can get everything you need at once but the items usually have an identifiable look that will help unify your decor no matter what room they turn up in.

- **A case for baskets.** Any room in Jen and Aaron's first floor can quickly transform from family room to entertaining area thanks to clever storage solutions. Bins are found everywhere—an elegant wire basket in the living room keeps the adults' books and magazines tidy, and plastic buckets under the bench seats in the addition can be used to quickly store crafts and toys.

THE
GREAT
WIDE
OPEN

Kara uses chapters from her life in her dynamic open-concept,
multi-functional converted-factory space   photography by Donna Griffith

Kara's amazing
collection of kilim
carpets helps to
map out where the
dining area ends
and the living
area begins.

K

ara Hamilton lives in a cool, converted warehouse. Built in 1914, the building retains many historic touches such as 12-foot-high beamed ceilings and huge windows.

Despite all the airiness, making a former industrial space feel like a snug and cheerful spot can be a challenge, but the artist and self-taught jewellery maker has created such an environment by using the same approach she takes to her assemblages: she brings objects and space together to create a narrative.

It also helps that many of her possessions are moveable. Rugs can be rolled up and put away. Her kitchen bar is on wheels so it can be easily relocated to create a workspace in another part of the loft. And a sliding barn door serves as a gallery wall and privacy screen between the sleeping space and the rest of the loft.

Kara's living space is a collage of colour, texture and history. Although many objects that furnish the home were inherited, "what makes it mine is in my curation," says Kara. It's about the narrative that she created between her space, her things and herself.

big box

Lofts are appealing because there's so much room to move, dance, create and live in. Sometimes, however, it can be tricky to furnish a big space. Here are three ways Kara made her floor plan fun and functional.

- **Let the sun shine in.** Because the loft is a corner unit, the room is lit by enormous windows. To further reflect the light, Kara painted the ceiling, floors and brick a warm white.

- **Where's the wall space?** While there are 12-foot walls, two of them have those huge windows. To create more vertical space, Kara acquired an almost floor-to-ceiling bookshelf and uses unconventional surfaces, such as a sliding door, to hang art on.

- **Use odd spaces.** Kara's condo has an L shape near the entrance that does double duty as a welcoming foyer for guests and a small office space for her.

BUCKET LIST

If your rooms do double duty, these storage sacks can help you compartmentalize your supplies without sacrificing style

project by Arounna Khounnoraj   photography by Donna Griffith

For quick cleanups, we want our things to be out of sight, not out of mind. Which is why we love the soft fabric storage buckets designed by Arounna from Bookhou. They're so pretty that you'll want to leave them out on display. They also let you organize your crazy collection of craft materials and other important bits.

MATERIALS

- 1 18"x7½" rectangle of printed canvas
- 1 18"x7½" rectangle of plain canvas (for the lining)
- 1 circle of printed canvas (6¾" diameter)
- 1 same-size circle of plain canvas

INSTRUCTIONS

1. Sew the short ends of the printed rectangle together (½" seam allowance), printed side in, creating a tube shape.

2. Sew one end of tube to printed circle, printed sides facing (½" seam allowance). Snip curved edge of resulting bucket bottom so seam sits flat.

3. Repeat steps 1 and 2 with the plain canvas rectangle and circle. This will be your liner.

4. Place the printed bucket into the liner bucket, with the "good" sides facing each other, so the top edges of the buckets align. Sew along this top edge, joining the two parts, but leave an opening of about 3". Use this opening to turn the bucket right side out. Fold in opening edges ½" and topstitch to close.

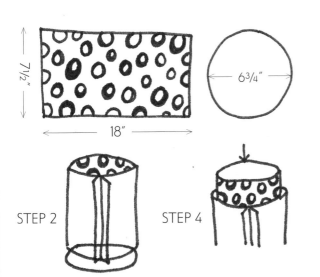

We like Arounna's bold, graphic patterns, so we decided to get crafty by making our own potato print shapes for our storage buckets. Here's how you can leave a big impression!

MATERIALS

- ½ potato per stamp
- fabric paint
- small sponge brush
- pen or fine-tip marker
- X-ACTO blade
- wax paper

INSTRUCTIONS

1. Wash potatoes thoroughly to remove any dirt and cut in half. Using a pen or fine-point marker, trace the design you want as your pattern onto the potato.

2. To make your stamp, cut away from the design you just drew, using the knife. These cuts need to be only about ¼" deep.

3. Place wax paper on your working surface before laying down your fabric. It will keep your surface clean, as paint can leak through fabric when stamping.

4. Pour fabric paint into a shallow dish or saucer. Using a small sponge brush, apply paint to stamp.

5. Slowly and firmly press stamp onto fabric, then lift stamp straight up and off fabric. Allow to dry.

In any good story, relationships are key. One thing we've learned over the years is that developing a meaningful relationship with your stuff is essential. What you collect throws some light on your interests and passions, but it's how you organize and edit your things that really tells the tale

LIVING WITH THE THINGS YOU LOVE

LYNDA LOVES LACE

And bugs and scales and paint-by-numbers. Her collections come together in the most charming home we know   photography by **Donna Griffith**

Many collections intersect in Lynda's living room. The kilim and the vintage yardsticks under the mantel are the most recent additions.

Wasp nests are a favourite of Lynda's and can be found throughout the house. "They're nature's papier mâché," she says.

WELCOME TO THE HOME of *Covet Garden* co-founder Lynda Felton. She has lived in this Leslieville row house for 13 years, surrounded by good neighbours, an amazing garden and a lively community.

Inside the house, she's surrounded by the most covetable collection of collections. Covetable because she has been acquiring her treasures since, well, forever. Since before old signage and taxidermy became impossible to find.

Lynda's likes are eclectic. She loves nature, so you'll find botanical drawings, specimens and finds such as feathers throughout her rooms. "I've always been drawn to natural history," she says. Some of her favourites are the old etchings over her mantelpiece. "Somebody saw these animals and had to reproduce them from memory. And they're beautiful!"

"I like to create a sense of happy abundance," says Lynda.

this page: Lynda is attracted to objects that have a use; then she finds another way to use them.

EVEN THOUGH she has many interests, they all weave together, thanks to careful collation. "It's better if you keep like things in groups or break them up into displays of one or two," says Lynda. Along one wall of her dining room are smaller collections, such as the mesh purses, which are family heirlooms. She had an uncle and aunt who were antique dealers and would send her a "Guess What This Is Present" every year. Sometimes she would be kept guessing for months as the gadgets and doodads were no longer in common use. The big jar filled with rusty metal tools on page 42 was her gift one year.

Lynda's dining room set is also an heirloom—it used to be the centrepiece of her grandmother's dining room, and she has wonderful memories of sitting around it, listening to her family share stories. However, she's not a big fan of red wood, so she painted the chairs white so the set would better integrate with the look of the rest of the house. "Adding some white makes a small place feel lighter and more spacious."

In the kitchen, you'll find many examples of her favourite collectible: scales. While it's hard for Lynda (or anybody) to pinpoint exactly what draws them to collect certain objects, she says that she is always attracted to anything that serves a function. "I admire pieces, like the scales, that actually work," Lynda says. "I love so many things, but my house is so small that everything has to be displayed in an interesting way or have a practical use."

SOME OF LYNDA'S BEST FINDS

are in almost every room of the house. Textured textiles such as bark cloth or artworks by friends (especially young artists like Maggie, age six, who lives across the street) provide a unifying thread from room to room.

Upstairs, the collections are even more personal. Family photos can be found throughout her bedroom alongside groupings of vintage lunchboxes and petrified mushrooms. The fungi are an extension of Lynda's admiration for all things organic, but the weathered tin boxes represent her love for reanimating old objects. "I like to hunt through the dusty old antique shops that everybody else is afraid to go into," she says. "The dirtier the better!"

Still, Lynda describes her bedroom as "girly." Her love of fabrics makes the space feel more feminine. She likes to show off her stash of vintage grain sacks and hand-crocheted tablecloths by using them as bed runners. It's also a peaceful place where she can surround herself with light and light textures. Her window faces east and welcomes the morning sun through floral curtains.

Lynda also loves girly things like necklaces and other jewellery finds from friends, family and souvenirs from trips to local shops and faraway places. While she doesn't always wear jewellery, she likes to display her collection on hooks fashioned from branches (made by her friend Katy's dad). "If I'm going to spend money on something," she says, "I want to see it."

opposite page:
Familiar faces are important to Lynda. Her most recent addition is a watercolour of her beloved pup, Lily.

"Maybe it was because my mom was a florist that I have to have flowers and plants in my life at all times," says Lynda.

Display is crucial to make collections come together.

VISITORS TO LYNDA'S will find un-expected and self-contained displays, such as the wall of paint-by-numbers artworks that follow you up the stairs. "I had a few, but in 2002 I went to the National Museum of American History's show on the history of paint-by-numbers and fell in love with them (and their story) even more," she says. "They all make me smile."

When she renovated her house to make the bathroom larger, Lynda designed it to function as a room that happened to have a bath in it rather than as a discrete space. So of course collections can be found here as well. It's a showcase for her love of birds and wire objects as well as a cup full of tiny baby dolls that sits on a shelf.

In her office, Lynda likes to be surrounded by things that spark creativity rather than specific sets of objects. But there are a few pieces that might inspire future collections, such as the tiger mask that was a gift from Matthew (whose apartment is also featured in this publication). "I said I loved it, and he gave it to me," says Lynda. "My things inspire me because they remind me of perfect moments in my life."

ALL TOGETHER NOW

An inveterate collector of textiles, cutlery and other ephemera, Matthew has used his magpie eye to build the coziest nest   **photography by Jodi Pudge**

What first made us fall in love with bookkeeper and designer Matthew Simpson's apartment was all the textiles, from the layers of well-loved bedding and old but adored carpets to the rich velvety sofa paired with sensible pillows.... Basically, we felt as snug as a bug in a rug as soon as we walked in the door.

Matthew's playful approach to print and pattern may be best described as patchwork. And the story of his space reflects this: the Victorian house was first a family home, then a rooming house, and later it was reorganized into apartments, one of them perfect to meet a single man's needs. His collections have been sourced from friends and junk stores ("but the junk-store owners prefer 'antique,' or worse, 'vintage store,'" says Matthew; "'vintage' is a word I do not like"). The pieces are organized to create something new, whole and original.

But there is also a deliberate method to Matthew's maximalism. He found his amazing abode by pounding the pavement in the neighbourhood he wanted to live in. "I was the eighth person to look at my apartment," he says. "I said to the landlord, if this was my place I'd never move, and he said, 'It's yours.'"

That determination also applies to Matthew's objects. Some of his collections come together easily because he's a fan of multiples, like the Fisher-Price Happy Apples, which are shelved on the wall near his fireplace. Another approach he takes to grouping objects is simply picking an empty area and filling it with related colours, patterns or themes.

Collecting, says Matthew, takes some effort. "Sometimes you don't find anything for years and then, BAM, you find four—and in the most obscure places." For example, he found one ALF doll and two Happy Apples at a Sunday flea market in Aachen, Germany. His wall of clocks took years to assemble. His favourite collection is his stash of cutlery. "None of it matches, but it all goes together," he says. "My friend designs cutlery, and he loves looking through it for interesting pieces."

textile on main street

We asked Matthew for some tips on collecting and incorporating preloved fabrics into your decor.

- **Mix and match.** "I'm a maximalist with both my home furnishings and my clothing."

- **Use the objects.** "I switch up the blankets and bedcovers and quilts in the winter."

- **Before you buy, ask a lot of questions** about the history, condition and provenance of an object— "especially from antique dealers and pickers." This info will not only help you care for the fabric, but also who doesn't love a good story?

- **Choose things you really like,** "not what a magazine or online source says is 'trending' (another word I dislike)."

- **Remember, you have to clean** fabrics as soon as you buy them.

Setting the scene:
A contemporary
black-and-white
piece by Canadian
artist Chris Curreri
is surrounded by
colourful folk art.

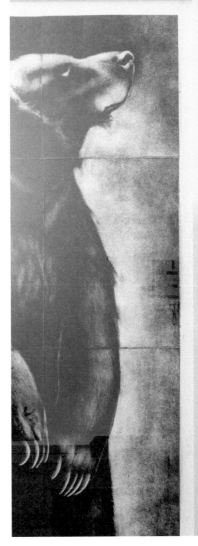

BEAUTIFUL MINDS

Janna and Dean honour history
while designing a better tomorrow
photography by Donna Griffith

The home of the architects Janna Levitt and Dean Goodman was built for change. They're committed to ideals of sustainability: to decrease waste, use green materials, increase density, limit unnecessary commuting and provide affordable housing. They also wanted to show that a modern space didn't need to feel cold and inaccessible. And they created a home demonstrating that all these ideals were not only possible but also desirable.

Part of the success of the space feeling so inviting is that it's filled with treasures from their own history as well as pieces from their parents and grandparents. The trick is in honouring heirlooms in a way that represents their own personalities. To keep things fluid, Janna and Dean value neutral interior architecture. "If the space had a specific style, you'd have to match furniture to the layout," says Dean. "The architecture of the building lets multiple things fit in. It's neutral, so you can put old and new together."

Another example of old and new coming together is the dining table and the liquor cabinet that both came from Janna's childhood home in Montreal. "My dad and his brothers had a furniture company, and they invested in another that made Scandinavian-style furniture." The low table in the front room came from Dean's parents' home in Vancouver. "You take them with you," says Janna. "Why wouldn't you?"

Throughout the house there are a variety of collections—including artwork, ceramics, photos, aboriginal basketwork and textiles. Some of them come from family, some from their own collecting. "We have a wide bandwidth of interests," says Janna, "but there's a consistency to the taste." Objects are carefully arranged by theme or texture or shape. That's Janna and Dean's secret for assembling an eclectic assortment of items for maximum appeal to both eye and mind.

55

research and development

One of the reasons we love Janna and Dean is that they're research nerds like us. Collections often begin with one object that has an emotional appeal, but knowledge is also power when you're creating your own compilation.

- **Read all about it.** A lot of Janna and Dean's collections come from family, but they are equally passionate about their budding collection of Inuit art. Among that big pile of bedside reads is *Tammarniit (Mistakes): Inuit Relocation in the Eastern Arctic, 1939–63*. Reading, not necessarily about art per se, provides a deeper context that allows even greater enjoyment of the objects.

- **Experience it.** You may not be able to afford to buy museum-quality examples of Inuit art, but you can visit a museum and study master works (which might help you identify a rare treasure when you see one at a yard sale).

- **Study the market.** Some collections are about quantity—having a whole wall of jadeite bowls, for instance, can create an arresting display. Others are about quality—having three outstanding pieces of hand-carved folk art from Quebec may be all you need to find meaning in your collection. Either way, follow collectors' groups and auction listings to look for deals on your objects of desire.

GROUPS OF HEAVEN

Melissa's many collections surprise and delight in every nook of her downtown loft

photography by Maya Visnyei

There's so much that enchants visitors to the Kensingston Market loft of design blogger (thesweetescape.ca) Melissa DiRenzo —the sky-high ceilings, the bold-patterned wallpaper, the stunning view of the city and her amazing rooftop retreat. There's so much wonder that we couldn't possibly show it all in these pages.

So we decided to focus on what really drew us into Melissa's space —her amazing collections. The open-concept abode is home to groupings of everything from old tins to milk-glass vessels. "My favourite is my plate wall," says Melissa. "Most are finds from thrift shops. My only real investment was committing to all the holes in the wall to hang them."

Melissa says she is more a scavenger than a collector. In fact, until she bought her loft five years ago, she generally moved every two years, so she travelled light with few possessions. She has always been passionate about decor, filing away pictures of great rooms (in the days before Pinterest) and dreaming of the time she could create her own space filled with finds that reflect different parts of her personality. So when she moved into her own home, she says, "I kind of went crazy.

"I never go shopping with something specific in mind," she says. "I don't know the history or value of pieces. I'll just go into a thrift shop and see something that sparks my imagination.

"A friend of mine once said, 'I love that every time I come over here, I see something that surprises and delights me.'"

group show

How Melissa puts it all together:

- **Group objects** in odd numbers of three, five, seven and so on.

- **Place collections against a neutral background** to keep the overall space from looking too busy.

- **Contrast is good.** "I like pairing old and new, or white against a dark background," says Melissa.

- **Keep some sort of colour palette in mind** for a small space. "I love turquoise and use it in a lot of places to help tie everything together."

- **Money shouldn't be an issue for collecting:** Melissa's groupings are often thrift- and yard-sale finds. What unifies them is some sort of strong graphic statement in the pattern, shape or colour.

Both Glen and Michelle come from a graphic design background, so advertising objects are of interest to them. These framed 1950s fitness posters are from Glen's uncle.

PERSONAL PIECES

Michelle and Glen's perfect collections prove that you needn't spend a lot of money to create a masterpiece

photography by **Valerie Wilcox**

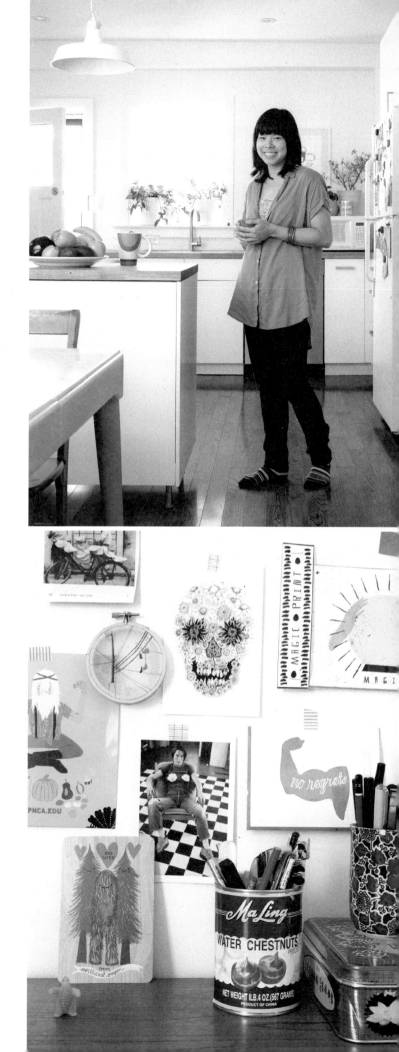

Massage therapist Michelle Yee and motorcycle enthusiast Glen Morrison live in one of the happiest homes that we've ever visited. It's not a big house, but it makes the most of its humble footprint, with light beaming in from the west, north and east—the place feels as if it was painted with a sunbeam. Michelle and Glen are a couple with a great sense of humour, and the design and layout of the house capture that light-heartedness.

A love of fun is also apparent in their collections. There's not a lot of stuff, but it's all interesting. There's a wall of vintage fans in an array of retro pastel colours. Handmade art and objects hang out casually with vintage antique shop and thrifted finds. And there's usually the spicy sweet scent of a freshly brewed pot of tea hanging in the air. It's like a walk-in welcome sign.

They have, at times, had to cull their cache. "The fan collection got out of hand," says Glen. "We had about 60 and now we're down to 20." Adds Michelle, "We could ask our friends to move only so many heavy boxes." One of the most wonderful benefits of the paring-down process was discovering that it doesn't take much to make a space more colourful and lively. Clearly, the couple are attracted to bold, graphic design and vibrant hues. The simplicity of the surroundings makes the vivid tones and patterns stand out, but it also keeps them in check, so nothing feels gaudy.

top left : "I really like the cubbyhole above our bed," Michelle says. It was a way to make an awkward wall into a usable space to store some of their books. And she also likes the "simple joy of the secret space."

editor's notes

- **Keep what's meaningful.** "We have stuff from my mom," says Michelle. "We have a lot of things from our youth. We're happy hobo hand-me-down people."

- **Reduce your footprint.** The couple travel a lot and pick up cards and postcards as souvenirs. These mini artworks make for an easy and inexpensive way to dress up a wall. In her office Michelle uses decorative washi tape to pin them to the wall for inspiration.

- **Everything in its place.** During their reno, says Michelle, "we took out so many walls that there was little space to put stuff. If an object didn't have a place, it was gone."

- **If it makes you happy, keep it.** Worry less about whether it's valuable or collectible and care more about what it contributes to your own story. Michelle admits that the reason she collects something can be entirely emotional. "I don't even sew and I have a fabric stash."

PAGE COUNTS

Designers are always talking about "curating a space," but here's how an actual curator assembled his collections **photography by Tracy Shumate**

Dennis Reid, an author, art historian and independent curator, lives surrounded by the things that he loves. His towering bookshelves teem with rare tomes that peek out from behind all kinds of stalks and fronds. His place reminds us of the way Max's room turns into a jungle in Maurice Sendak's *Where the Wild Things Are*.

When he started searching for a new place to live, he had three conditions: he wanted to be close to the University of Toronto, where he's a professor in the art history department, and to the Art Gallery of Ontario, where he was the chief curator at the time; he needed room for his books; and he had to have space for his plants. Fortunately he found a two-storey loft conversion that not only allowed him to amass a wall of literature but also provided a light-filled space for his greeneries to grow as tall as they wanted.

His roots in Canadian art also run deep in the space. Works by friends like Greg Curnoe, Michael Snow and others inhabit the rooms of his home. The roominess of the space also allows Dennis to display some of the ephemera of his life, such as the arrowhead collection he found as a boy; it began his interest in archaeology and ultimately led him to art history.

In fact, almost every piece in the place has a personal history. "My mom and dad were veteran antique market prowlers—a lot of the glass objects you see here come from them." One of the most interesting things about Dennis's objets is that they're all in use. For example, decorative glass jar lids serve as paperweights on his desk. "At this point, things have to have a function," he says. "I'm not interested in cluttering the space up."

magic carpets

Another of Dennis's collections is old carpets (a passion he was introduced to by his late friend the abstract painter David Bolduc). These beauties see everyday use. Here are some tips to maintaining vintage carpets.

• **Reduce UV-ray damage** with shading or a protective window coating. Exposure to intense sunlight is not good for textiles.

• **Take care of spills or spot stains immediately**, using a moist, clean cloth to blot (don't scrub) from the edges toward the centre of the spill. If you need soap, use shampoo, as the protein of wool is similar to human hair. Then elevate the

damp area on a short stool or box for quick air-drying.

• **Vacuum frequently** to remove dust and silt, which wear the pile down under foot traffic. Small kilims can be brushed. For older pieces, use a low suction setting or opt for a non-electric sweeper (regular cleaning is also your best insurance against moth damage).

• **Rotate your carpets** at least every two years so traffic is spread out evenly.

• **Have your carpets hand-washed** or tumbled by a professional cleaner every four to six years.

LIGHT SHOW

A clever way to shine a
spotlight on your favourite
examples of children's art

project by Iza Mokrosz

photography by Donna Griffith

Parents collect more of their kids' artwork than they can possibly hold on to or hang on their walls. Artist Iza Mokrosz came up with this great way to honour your kids' creativity and display pieces around your home in a new way!

MATERIALS
- some of your kids' favourite artwork
- existing paper lampshade
- utility knife
- metal ruler
- white glue

INSTRUCTIONS

1. At a local copy shop transfer the artwork onto UV Ultra paper or another paper that has a similar translucency to it. Iza made 30 copies of the artwork.

   HINT: You can have colour images printed as black-and-whites if you want to unify the effect.

2. Using the utility knife and the metal ruler, cut the copies into 2"x2" squares. For variety, Iza made squares in both horizontal and diagonal orientations.

3. Working from the top of the paper lampshade, begin attaching the squares with glue. Apply a tiny dot to the top corner of each square and, aligning the squares on the diagonal, affix the first row to the shade.

4. Glue down the second row, placing each new square between two on the row above, with the top ones overlapping slightly—making a pattern similar to that of a pineapple.

5. Continue down until you have completely covered the length of the lampshade.

STEP 3a
(view of top
of lampshade)

STEP 3b

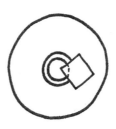

HINT: Use a low-energy bulb to save power and reduce the amount of heat emitted from the bulb and therefore any potential fire hazard.

How you organize your home and its functions can help provide structure for your own story—especially when it comes to integrating life and work. With a little care (and some clever design tips), you can bring the two together visually and build practical boundaries at the same time

MAKING SPACE FOR LIFE AND WORK

MAKER STYLE

Craftspeople John and Arounna are reinventing the idea of the local business by combining storefront, studio and home **photography by Ashley Capp**

opposite: Arounna and John in the studio space at the back of the ground floor.
this page: Having living and workspace on separate floors helps delineate spaces for business and pleasure. Using the living room to showcase John's furniture ties the spaces together.

"Our kitchen is mostly IKEA," says Arounna. "We try to strike a balance between doing things ourselves and being realistic."

ONLY A FEW GENERATIONS ago the

shops that line Dundas Street West were always multi-purpose places. Shop owners would live above their boutiques with their families. And many shops manufactured their own goods on the premises. When John Booth and Arounna Khounnoraj, designers and craftspeople, bought their building, they brought that tradition back to the street.

Together they own the multidisciplinary studio Bookhou. "Because we make things," says Arounna, "we really wanted to have a storefront." They were also looking for studio space as well as a building that could house their family (son Liam and daughter Piper). A practical pair, they decided to invest in a place where they could not only create and sell their wares but where the kids could also roam freely—a crucial necessity if you want to spend quality time with the family and run a small business.

"We like the idea of our being here in the shop," she continues. "We like that people can see work." Because they are creative, and because of the way they create, John and Arounna have no problem with combining craft, commerce and family. "We like making things," says Arounna. "We sort of intuitively do things together."

This philosophy explains the duo's spare but sunny aesthetic. There's a mix of found and inherited objects along with John and Arounna's own designs. But there are few things that aren't useful or well considered. As craftspeople, says Arounna, "we're interested in quality materials. We got a claw-foot bathtub after looking at cheaper vinyl tubs. We thought, will we be happy with a vinyl tub in five years?"

They believe in investing in the idea of working from home and keeping manufacturing alive in their community. Since we first visited the family, they have been constructing an addition so John can get his studio out of the basement to work on larger projects. "Originally it was a house," says John of their beloved building. "At some point someone put a box in the front and a box in the back. This building is always in a state of becoming," he says.

BOOKHOU
SHOP HOURS
WED. 11-5
THU.-SAT. 11-6
SUN. 12-5

all in the family

When you have kids, working from home can be a blessing. You can save money on childcare, you get to spend time with your kids, and as John and Arounna have found, your family can also serve as a constant source of inspiration. But merging work and play can be challenging. Here's how to find a balance.

- **Don't be too precious.** Kids will want to be in any room that you're in, so supply some kid-friendly zones in your workspace. "There's a chalkboard wall in my studio," says Arounna, "and there's a chalkboard table." She also likes to kid around. "I like it that you can have a thought and just write it down."

- **Minimize stuff.** Says Arounna, "We do try to keep the number of toys down. We're very minimalist. If it's not going to be used, it's not going to be there."

- **Let it flow.** "We chose this place because of the central staircase," says John. "The kids can come down when we're working and hang out with us."

Shop snapshot:
The view from John and Arounna's shop, Bookhou. It's important to them that passersby can see that things are being made on the premises.

Woodsy materials (and big new windows) link the interior of the house to the backyard studio.

LOVE CONNECTION

A few new windows and an ingenious backyard landscaping design redefine the concept of work and home   photography by Maya Visnyei

opposite: The studio workspace as seen from the house.
this page: Deanne (left) and Christina hanging out by their new firepit.

We once heard Christina Zeidler and Deanne Lehtinen called "partners in art and love," and we had to steal that description as it's so perfect. On paper, they have very different jobs (Christina is a visual artist, filmmaker, musician and is also the developer and president of the Gladstone Hotel, and Deanne is a furniture designer/ builder), but they collaborate on some pretty cool art projects and exhibitions such as a lampshade made of vintage sunglasses.

Their Parkdale house is a partnership of another kind. A stable-turned-studio serves as Christina's workspace, but it's furnished with Deanne's work and the couple's combined projects. Christina loves working from home (Deanne's studio is just around the corner) because even when they're busy, they still see each other. "My favourite place in the studio is by the window so I can wave at Deanne when she's on the deck or in the house."

The studio is where bandmates and friends also come together to work on even more projects. For example, Christina just finished filming a feature, and the studio served as a production office with a 40-person crew coming in and out at all hours.

Which is why it was critical to create an outdoor space that not only linked the two buildings but also provided some distance. They enlisted friend Todd Caldwell of Emblem Floral Studio to help them synthesize a design that provided access between the buildings but used terraces and plantings to create more private areas as well. "It's great because Christina works on so many collaborative projects," says Deanne, "so there's a separation for me as well."

The two-level studio space is designed to be as flexible as possible to support its many uses (it also serves as a rehearsal space for Christina's band, a guest house and a cat-free zone). "Because it's a separate space, it feels like I'm going to my job," says Christina. "It surprised me how easily it let me separate work and home."

office space

For Christina and Deanne, having visual stimulation inspires their work and their art. So when it came to home improvements, "we wanted to make sure that every view was a great view," says Deanne. Here's how to quickly improve your office outlook.

- **Set up near a window.** Christina loves her desk. "Writing is tough sometimes," she says, "but whenever I look out the window there's something going on. Just watching the squirrels running around makes me feel energized."

- **Multi-purpose.** One of Christina's favourite pieces of furniture is "a crazy old oak table that rolls around that was a relic from the Gladstone." Because it's on wheels, it can serve several uses within the

space, but it can also be wheeled out of the way when it's not needed.

- **Surround yourself with stuff you love.** Sometimes it just takes a glimpse of a favourite object to take you to your happy place on a stressful workday. "I love Deanne's stage cord macramé lamp," says Christina. "My favourites are the Keith Cole for Mayor posters in the bathroom," says Deanne.

- **Make distractions.** If you have a dilemma that you just can't resolve, it can help to step outside of work for a minute. When she was working on her film, Christina and her cinematographer pitched a tent inside the studio and lit up *The Fire Box* (shown above) to create a temporary work-free zone.

HOME WORK

Artist, illustrator and designer Alanna
believes in making the world a more
beautiful place, starting with her home

photography by Jodi Pudge

PENGUIN
BOOKS

A ROOM OF
ONE'S OWN

VIRGINIA WOOLF

SERVICES EDITION

COMPLETE   UNABRIDGED

A quick look around Alanna's loft reveals how her surroundings influence her work (those are her silkscreened book covers, shoe and scissors hanging on the wall).

opposite page:
Alanna surrounds
herself with books
for inspiration. "Books
are so important to
me," she says. "If I go
into a house without
books, I kind of feel
like leaving."

Most people require a dedicated space plus a desk and computer in order to work from home. Artist and illustrator Alanna Cavanagh needs that to run her business, and she needs a whole lot more room to make her silkscreens, store her prints and work. Perhaps this is why she describes her studio/living space as "in transition."

When Alanna moved into her building in Toronto's west end three years ago, she was flummoxed by the amount of space. "My friend and interior designer Kim Flaherty was the first person to see it, and it was her idea to make a very wide entranceway," she says. "It was a great idea as it feels very welcoming—especially when clients come over."

Having so much space presented another challenge when it came to integrating Alanna's workspace with her lifestyle. "It's great for turning around my bike and parking it with ease," she says, but sometimes the studio threatened to take over the living space. Until recently, she had her office alongside a wall of windows next to her living room but then moved it to a nook outside of her bedroom. "I like enclosed, cavelike spaces," she says. "And before, I always had the curtains drawn so I could see the screen. As a result, her living room doubled in size and became a place where she could remove herself from deadlines when she needed to.

Truth be told, Alanna loves her work and doesn't mind when her dining table needs to turn into a workspace or that her office doesn't have a view. "I don't think it's a problem. I like having the wall space so I can put up pictures and things that inspire me.

"And if I have to get away from work, I have a great boyfriend who has a fabulous space," she says.

beautiful work

Alanna believes that everybody deserves a beautiful workspace. She's all for devoting a part of each day to straightening, decorating and generally prettying up her office and studio. Here are three ways she improved her workflow.

- **Choose the right furniture.** "I've never met an L desk I didn't like," says Alanna: its two areas can be used to stage separate projects and avoid confusion.

- **Divide and conquer.** "My illustration office is just a computer, a scanner and a printer," says Alanna. "I like to keep it neat and tidy. My silkscreen area is inky and messy and needs a ton of space." Having a division between the two helps keep the two worlds from falling into chaos.

- **Have a place for everything.** Even though Alanna will use her dining table to work on prints, once they're dry, they're safely put away into storage cabinets. Likewise, books are reshelved according to use. "The bookshelf in the living room is for Alanna the person. The shelf outside my office is for Alanna the artist. I consider them my school."

Alanna's dining table does double duty as a print-making surface.

Art is important in Victoria's life and serves as inspiration in every room of the house—including this image by Toronto-based artist Claire Greenshaw in the kitchen.

EMPLOYMENT HISTORY

A woman of many talents, Victoria needed to create a space where she felt at home working, entertaining and just hanging out photography by Jodi Pudge

below right: Victoria is also active in community gardening initiatives such as this urban rooftop garden above a local restaurant.

Landscape architect Victoria Taylor is a collaborator by nature. She works closely with clients to create thoughtful green gardens. She also works in concert with designers and artists to make spaces that feel alive and energetic. And she's a firm supporter of her community and works with many groups to hold fundraising events in her Queen West neighbourhood.

It's natural, then, that her space is a collaboration between work (she meets with clients in her spacious main-floor kitchen but keeps her study separate and private on the second floor), her community service (she holds fundraising events in her home that spill out into her amazing backyard), and her quiet times hanging out with friends (serving low-key dinner and drinks around almost banquet-size tables in her dining room and on the patio).

At the same time, she says, "I don't want my whole house to be a workspace." Layout helps define the space to suit her needs. While the main floor is mostly open concept, which makes it feel big enough for entertaining a large group, there are defined uses within the space, which helps it feel more intimate when one simply wants to relax.

Victoria also emphasizes the contribution of music and art in defining different areas. Music is important and her collection of records helps the space transition from business in the front to party in the back. Being surrounded by art is one joy of working from home for Victoria. Having access to the natural world—especially her garden—also provides inspiration. "Now that I'm working from home I'm more aware of the space at different times of the day."

inspiration stations

When you work from home, distractions can sometimes provide inspiration.

- **Take a break.** "Music is a huge part of my life," says
Victoria. When she needs a break to clear her head,
she listens to some LPs in her front room.

- **Keep your focus.** Victoria doesn't stress about making her home a showcase of her designs: it's a place
she can relax. "I focus my design energy on my work."

- **Mixing it up is important.** If you assumed that
because she's a landscape architect, Victoria's
home would be more of a jungle inside, you would
be mistaken. "I work with materials such as steel
and concrete and wood," she says. "Plants are just
part of the palette."

- **Consider all of your senses** when creating a workspace that you love to be in. In Victoria's office,
we literally stopped to smell the pages of a vintage
publication. Guess what, old books smell terrific!

SMALL BUSINESS

Stephanie and Samuel have created a harmonious balance between work and home in a 550-square-foot apartment **photography by Valerie Wilcox**

Because it's such a small space, Stephanie and Samuel's collections focus on small items such as vintage found photographs and bottles that were discovered on amateur digs in the countryside.

Perched on the third floor of a century house in Parkdale is the tiniest space we've ever photographed. It's the home of interior designer Stephanie Pellatt and her husband, construction project manager Samuel Cerizza. We're familiar with such rental units, we've even lived in a few, but when we walked into this walkup our jaws dropped. It's almost like a magic trick how they managed to combine a working home office with a welcoming living room in only 550 square feet of floorspace.

Stephanie and Sam met in Spain, and, after some years of a long-distance relationship, married in his native Italy. Stephanie returned to Canada while Samuel organized his move, and she searched for an inexpensive but practical apartment so they could save up money. She found the top-floor rental on Craigslist. "It looked really bad," says Stephanie, "but I could see this amazing arched ceiling, and I was happy that nobody else was competing with me."

The apartment still has many original architectural features, such as a fireplace, mouldings and windows. Because there are only four rooms in the apartment (including a walk-in-closet-size kitchen, a bath and a good-size bedroom), the biggest challenge was incorporating her office into what was already a combination living/dining space. But Stephanie was able to use the design of the vaulted ceiling to help define where her workspace would be. Basically, the living and dining areas follow the arch while the workspace fits into an alcove. An IKEA bookcase turned on its side separates the two spaces. "It lets me store my stuff so it doesn't bleed into the living space." Not only does this shelf house Stephanie's many reference books and project files, it also doubles as a workspace and as an additional eating counter when they entertain.

Another way Stephanie and Samuel integrate their work and living space is by keeping their furnishings portable. They reached their current configuration "piece by piece," says Stephanie. Their sectional is actually an outdoor sofa. It's sturdy but lightweight enough that it can easily be reconfigured into a guest bed for visitors. The rest of the furnishings, she says, "are a mix of found, antiques, gifts, garage-sale finds or hand-me-downs."

paint it black (or white)

When your workspace is out in the open, you can use colour to integrate it with the rest of your rooms.

- **Off-white.** To help create a visual flow between rooms, an off-white palette was picked up in accessories in the bathroom, kitchen (for example, the mixing bowls, pictured right) and bedroom.

- **Grey-blue white.** Stephanie drew out the architectural features such as the fireplace and trim with a slightly different white, one with a subtle tint of grey-blue to look crisp.

- **Shiny black.** To unify the look of the found furniture, she used black exterior enamel paint ("just make sure you apply it in a well-ventilated area").

- **Textured white.** To keep her office wall organized, she painted a pegboard wall behind her computer white to blend with the rest of the decor.

The kids
can relax
on couches
covered with
Heather's
creations.

COTTAGE INDUSTRY

Instead of bringing her work home, Heather brings homeyness to her work

photography by Donna Griffith

Heather collects vintage textiles, which she likes to use for inspiration.

Sometimes it feels as if urbanites are just as startled to discover that people still manufacture things in the city as they would be to find a chicken house in their neighbour's backyard. We were surprised and delighted to discover that textile artist Heather Shaw runs her home furnishing business, Pi'Lo, in a converted coach house (and former sausage factory) behind their Trinity Bellwoods home—a workshop that combines her neighbourhood's tradition of industry with a relaxing rural aesthetic.

In her work, Heather aims to create objects responsibly in the hope that they'll be passed down from generation to generation. This objective means that she tries to incorporate as many natural fabrics and finishes as possible into her space.

The natural touches link the studio and the house together visually, and wicker baskets and ceramic jars also help keep her workspace organized. "I'm a big believer in baskets," says Heather.

And when work requires expansion, she's able to adapt her house to suit that need. For example, the kitchen counter is a double-wide one. "When I have to fill a larger order," says Heather, "I hire a group of women to help package everything. It's like having a quilting bee.... We make a pot of tea, gather round the table and have these interesting conversations."

business plans

Working from home is the dream, but it's still work. "You have to separate the two," says Heather. Here's how to figure out if a home studio is right for you.

- **Consider the financial costs.** "I used to work at a studio at Queen and John," says Heather, "but I did the math, and making a studio here worked out to be the same financially."

- **Keep it simple.** Heather also saved money (and keeps work distractions to a minimum) by having functional and spare furnishings in her workspace. Basic shelving is used to organize supplies, and an old folding table serves as a workstation.

- **Make it pleasing.** Include attractive small touches such as a table lamp, vases filled with blooming branches or a couple of antique tins that suggest a picnic in a sylvan glade waits just outside the door.

103

HANG IN THERE

Take a little extra time out of your workday to create this wonderful wall caddy   photography by **Donna Griffith**

The beautiful part about this organizer is that you can customize it to be any size you like. We made our caddy 20"x30" (not including the hanging tabs), but if you have a smaller space, or want to store wee items such as jewellery or art supplies, feel free to downsize (or supersize).

MATERIALS

- fabric—you'll need it to be three times the size of your caddy. For example, our caddy is 20"x30", so we used a 60"x90" piece of fabric. The extra fabric will be used to create the storage pockets.
- coordinating thread
- straight pins
- paper
- pencil
- scissors
- iron
- wood dowel (cut to the width of your caddy plus 4")

INSTRUCTIONS

1. From your fabric, cut two panels to your desired size (again, we used 20"x30" panels). These will be your front and back panels.

2. On each side of each panel, fold the edge under about ¼" and press flat.

3. Set one panel piece aside for your back panel.

4. The front panel fabric will be used to add patch pockets. With the paper and pencil, draw templates for your pockets based on your specific needs. For example, do you need to store mail? If so, cut a template the size of an envelope and then add an extra ¼" around the template for seam allowance. Using this method, create templates of various sizes to hold what you need.

5. Pin the paper templates onto the remaining (non-panel) fabric and cut out the desired pocket shapes.

6. Turn over a ¼" seam allowance on each side of pockets and press.

7. Topstitch all four sides of the pockets.

8. Arrange the patch pockets on the front panel fabric until you have the placement you like. Then pin the pockets onto the caddy. Sew three sides of the pockets to the panel, leaving the tops open.

9. Continue until all pockets are sewn into place. Stitch any dividers for pencils, pens or rulers after the pocket is sewn to front fabric. Simply stitch from the bottom of the pocket to the top in the width you prefer.

10. Pin the back panel to the front panel—good sides facing. Stitch caddy together, leaving the top open. Turn sewn caddy right side out.

11. Make a paper template for your hanging tabs. Our tabs were 6"x2¼". We cut five of them.

12. Pin the paper tab templates to the remaining fabric and cut out each shape. Then fold under a ¼" seam allowance down the length of each side of the tabs. Iron flat, then topstitch.

13. Fold each tab in half lengthwise, then pin along the top of the caddy, between the front and back panels, leaving a space of about 2" between tabs.

14. Topstitch straight across the top of the caddy, securing each tab in place.

15. Add dowel and hang.

Covet Garden couldn't happen without the creativity of our photographers. Here, our contributors show us how they see design through the camera's lens and in their own personal favourite spaces.

ashley capp
ashleycapp.com

We can't get enough of Ashley Capp's bright, light and crisp images. Her work has appeared in the *Globe and Mail*, *House and Home* and *Style at Home*. She's a fan of both food and design, and that undisguised delight in her subject matter really shows in her photos.

"I've had the opportunity to photograph great spaces and meet some fantastic people through *Covet Garden*. One of my most favourite spaces is Todd and Caitlin's family home. It had such a warm and inviting no-fuss feel to it, not to mention one of the most interesting workspaces I've shot!"

Ashley's favourite *Covet Garden* shoot was Caitlin, Todd and Emmett's family-friendly home featured in Issue 35.

'I SEE BEAUTY IN LIGHT AND SIMPLICITY '

'THERE IS NO LIFE IN A ROOM WITHOUT PERSONAL ELEMENTS'

donna griffith
donnagriffith.com

Decor fans should be very familiar with Donna's richly coloured and carefully composed images, as her work has appeared in magazines all over North America. Her own decor style is inspired in part by the spaces she shoots ("It's a professional hazard," she says). In fact, she adds, "Our whole kitchen reno, my 'girl cave' decor, our cabin reno" took elements from past shoots.

The key is adapting inspiration to tell your own story through decor. "Whether it's a collection of headless dolls as in Nancy Tong's home or singing pickles such as the one Olga Korper keeps in her kitchen, or Kara Hamilton's 'objets' from her parents' home, there is no soul without personal objects."

It's the thought that people put into their decor that also counts. "I love the privilege of being welcomed into someone's home and spending a day in the midst of a beautifully crafted space and in the company of the creative souls who live there."

clockwise from top left: Gallery owner Olga Korper's living room from Issue 15; Matthew and Jade's dining room from Issue 19; and Nancy and Laas's collections from Issue 14.

'I LIKE PEEKING INTO PEOPLE'S LIVES'

jodi pudge
jodipudge.com

While Jodi is best known for her food photography, we find the way she shoots spaces just as—if not more—scrumptious. She seems to easily focus on ingredients of a room that make it come alive.

"It's exciting to see what people choose to surround themselves with. When I'm finished shooting, it's as though I've gotten to know them over a much longer period of time."

Jodi and her partner, Jordan, are newish homeowners, and one of the things that working with *Covet Garden* has taught her, she says, is that a place doesn't need to be decorated in "typical" fashion or theme. "I'm inspired most just to fill our home with things that we love."

clockwise from top left:
Dani and Stefano's kitchen from Issue 20; tea-cups from Shelley and Brendon's place in Issue 2; Michael's sewing room and bedroom from Issue 32.

tracy shumate
tracyshumate.com

Tracy is like a sculptor in photography because her images explore the space around an object almost as much as the object itself.

"I shoot a lot of product. I like to investigate the beauty of each item and I like contrasts," she says. She also likes to explore life and has pursued many interests, including past gigs working in vintage clothing stores and coffee shops.

Because Tracy moves around a lot, her own spaces tend toward the minimalist. Her favourite things are usually sourced from what she finds on long ambles with her dog, Dusty. "As much as I like my stuff, I've thought about selling everything but me and the dog."

Tracy shot her own light-filled live/work space for Issue 6.

'I DON'T LIKE THINGS THAT ARE PERFECT'

maya visnyei
mayavisnyei.com

Maya is known for her work's refined simplicity. She is able to find the grace notes—the thoughtful and elegant details—in any space she photographs. Which is why her favourite *Covet Garden* shoot is Morgan and Christopher's home. "Their taxidermy collection made such an impression on me and was such a pleasure to photograph," says Maya. "I really liked how well the taxidermy pieces were curated so as to give the space its museum-like yet casual feel."

In her own world, her favourite place is "the client area" in her studio, which is home to an oversize armchair. She loves to settle into the chair after a long day of work. "Clients enjoy it as well," she says. "I've seen it hold five children at once, and even two grown adults managed to squeeze into it. I think people just see it and it somehow makes them feel at home in the studio."

clockwise from top left: A honey shoot from Issue 39, Morgan and Christopher's apartment from Issue 34 and a cool drink from Issue 20.

'IT'S THE SIMPLE THINGS IN LIFE THAT GIVE US THE MOST PLEASURE'

'I GET IDEAS ON SHOOTS
AND TRY TO FIT THEM
INTO MY OWN DECOR'

valerie wilcox
valeriewilcox.ca

Valerie brings a fine eye for detail to her photography. Her images make use of the little elements—the way a book is placed lovingly on a shelf, or a backgammon set is almost hidden under a credenza—that help colour a story.

She also likes to take these details and use them in her own home: "I find myself asking, 'Where did you get that?' multiple times when I'm on a *Covet Garden* shoot."

At the moment her favourite object is a sculptural piece by artist Holly Wheatcroft (from Issue 22) that was a gift to her new baby. "It's a white cloud that goes perfectly in his room."

images on left:
Details from the home
of ceramicist Xenia
Taler from Issue 24.
images on right:
Artist Holly's house
from Issue 22.

laura brown
proofreader/fact checker

Laura is a freelance editor and former curator. Her many projects include Iris Nowell's *Painters Eleven: The Wild Ones of Canadian Art.* A full-time mother of three, she has still managed to catch all our copy errors since the beginning of *Covet Garden*, and we love her for it.

arounna khounnoraj
project page 34

Arounna's designs investigate pattern and image in her textiles and sculptures. With her husband, John Booth, she founded Bookhou in 2002 to showcase their individual and collaborative multidisciplinary designs. They specialize in hand-made natural materials and small production pieces.

kim latreille
print co-ordinator

Kim is a publishing veteran who has produced some of Canada's best magazines, including *Cottage Life*, *Fashion* and *Toronto Life*. She's super pleased to add *Covet Garden* to her list. Kim lives in Toronto's Beach community with her two sons and her big fluffy dog, T-Bone.

iza mokrosz
project page 70

Iza's practice includes photography, drawing and painting, performance, sculpture and installation. Her most recent projects also explore the artist's relationship to various personal and familial artifacts and objects.

Iza's home appeared in Issue 23.

alison reid
copy editor

Alison, longtime editor and treasured *Covet Garden* contributor, has been with us since our first issue. She has also worked on fiction and non-fiction for various Canadian publishers.

thank you!

Anne Denoon
Kirk Elliot
Jennifer Flores
Matt Hilliard-Forde
Andrew Kines
Jasmine Miller
Luc Montpellier
Sarah Pickering
Andrew Rosen
Sarah Samms
Craig David Wallace
Melony Ward
Denise Wright-Ianni

Covet Garden Home wouldn't have been possible without the generous contributions of the following people:

Emma Bennett
Monique Bidal
Julia Breckenreid and Ryan Feeley
Laura Brown
Dali Castro
Don Corbett
Tiffany Dekel
Catherine Doherty
Todd Doldersum, Caitlin O'Reilly, Emmett & Ned
Millie Felton
Cheryl Forsley
Pilar Garcia
Alvaro Goveia
Daniel Harrison
Denise Hawk
Alexandra Hooper
Michael Humphries
Arti Kaushal
David Kines
Dawne Kissack-Pyke
KOKITO
Rosemary Little
Jasmine Miller
Jessica McEwen, Periwinkle Flowers

Colleen Nicholson
Eleanor Pearson
Stephanie Pellatt
Pistil Flowers
Jenn Playford
Jodi Pudge
Alison Reid
Dennis Reid
Gloria Reid
Mia Ena Risojevic
The Roy (Mark & Andy)
Molly Seon
Shed The Eclectic Home (Cindy Potters)
Victoria Smith
SouthEnd Farm & Vineyards
Anna-Maria C Sviatko
Sweet Bliss Baking Company
Shelley van Benschop
Maya Visnyei
Jayne Whyte
Denise Wright-Ianni, CGA Prof. Corp.
Manuela Yarhi
Cybèle Young
Nicole Young

Alanna
Cavanagh

Illustration
Prints
Surface Design

Katy Dockrill

KATYDOCKRILL.COM